# Art

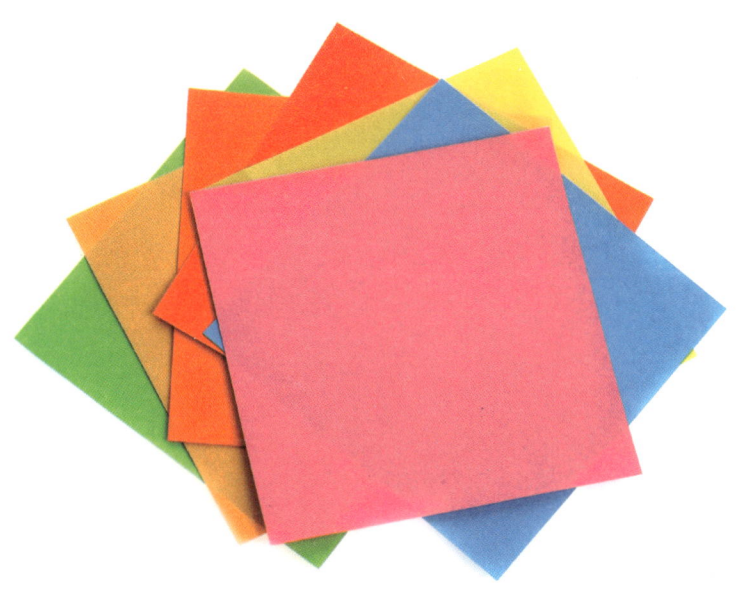

Seed
Learning

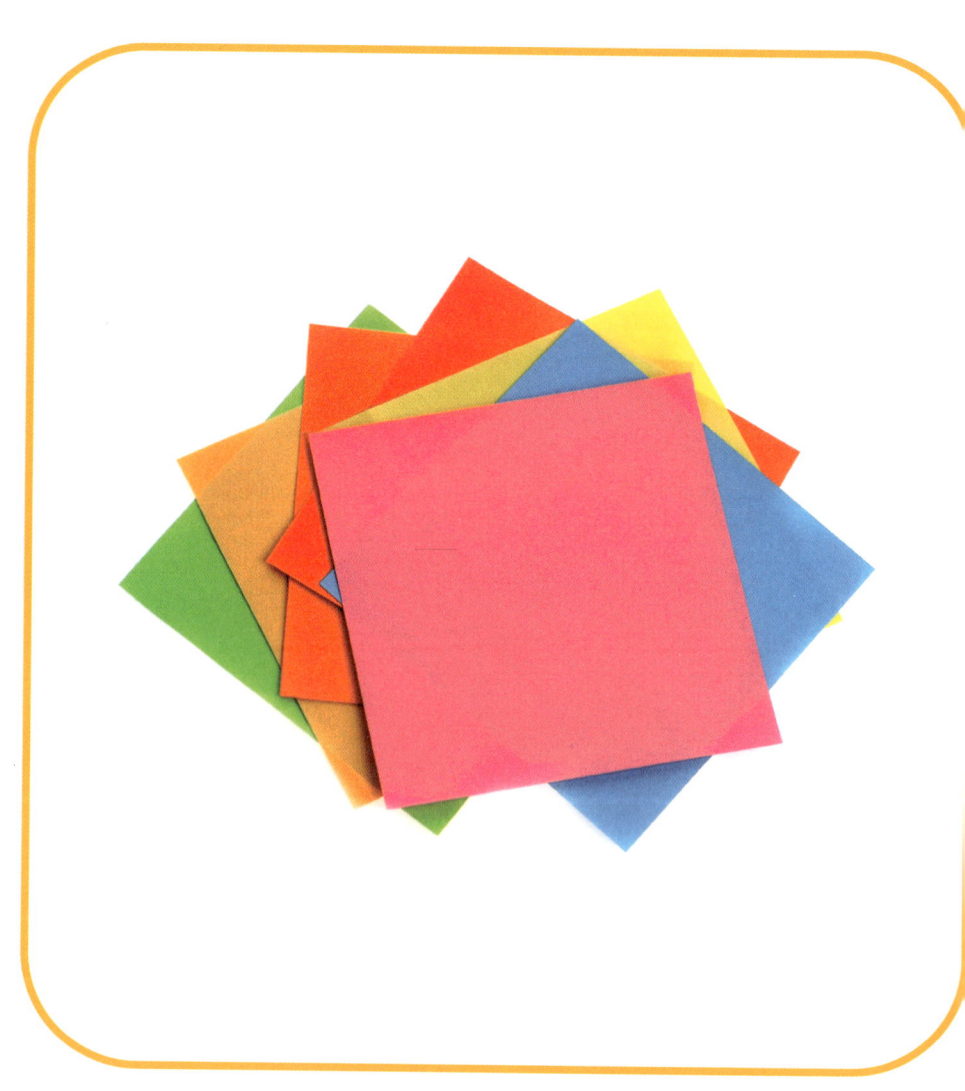

# paper

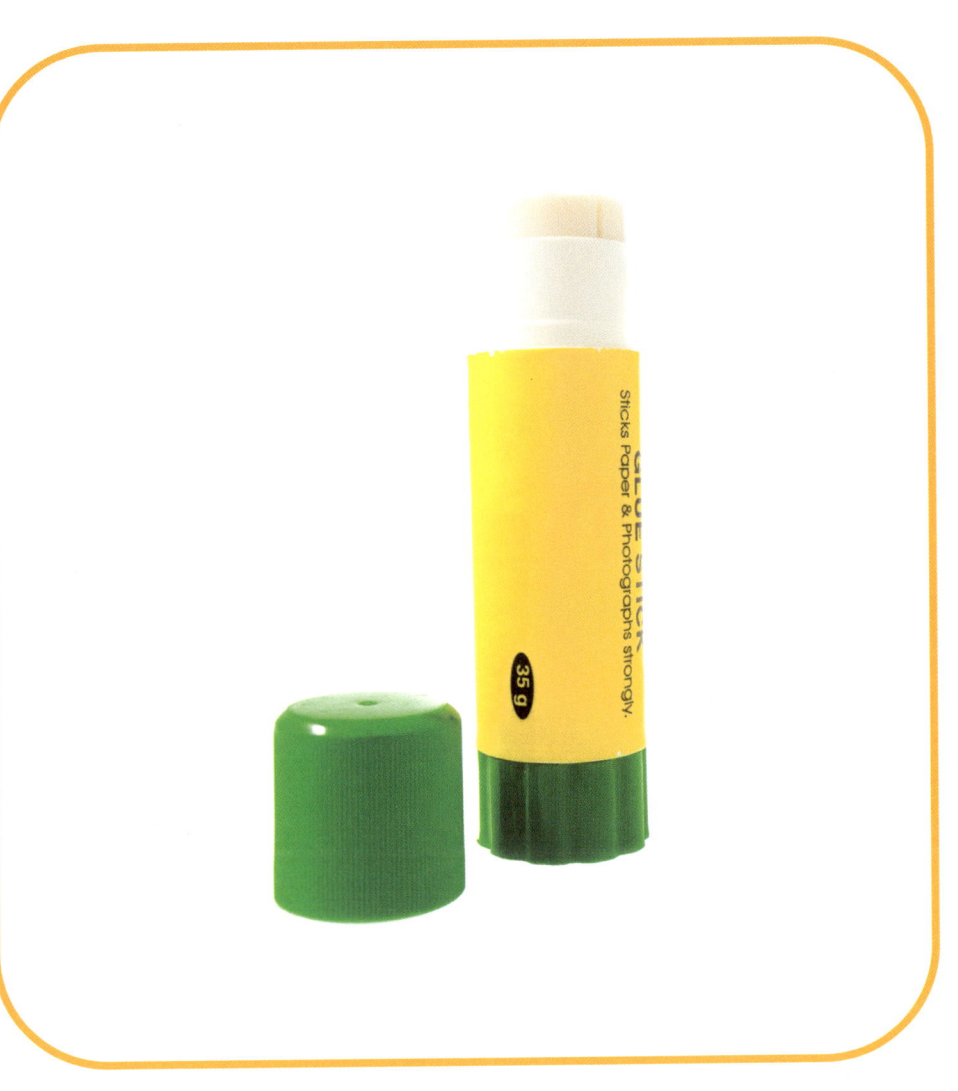

# glue

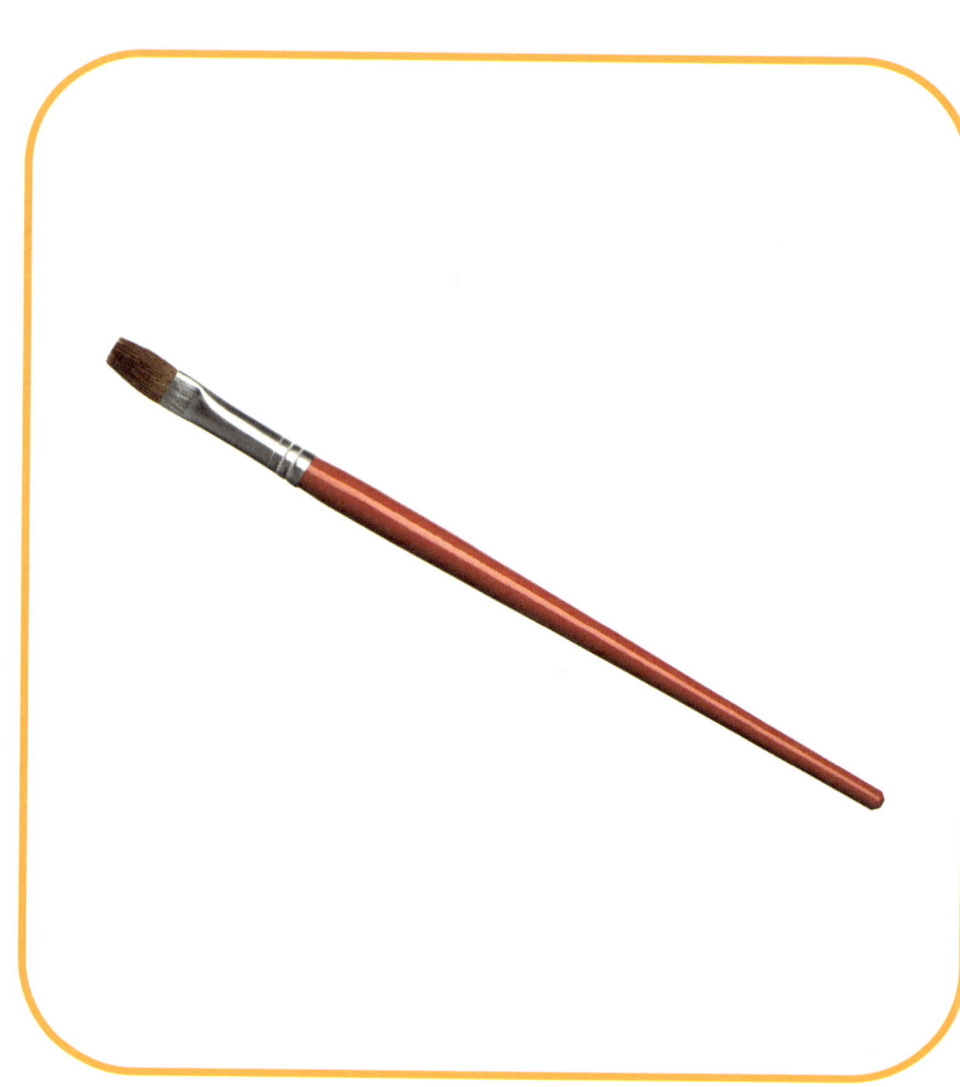

# brush

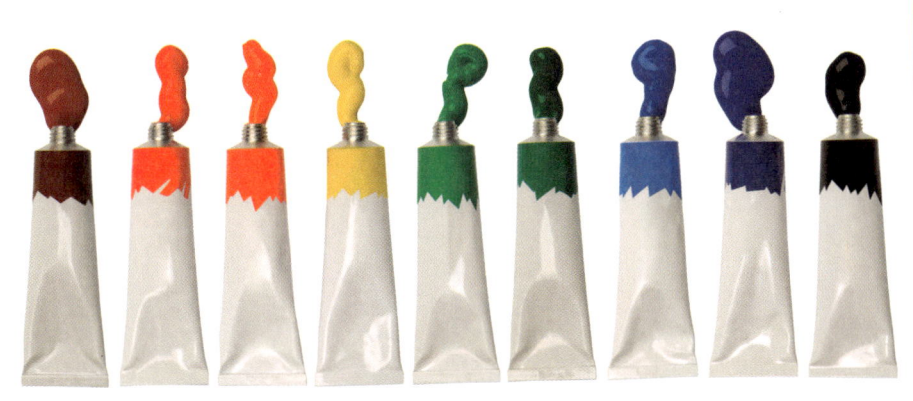

paint

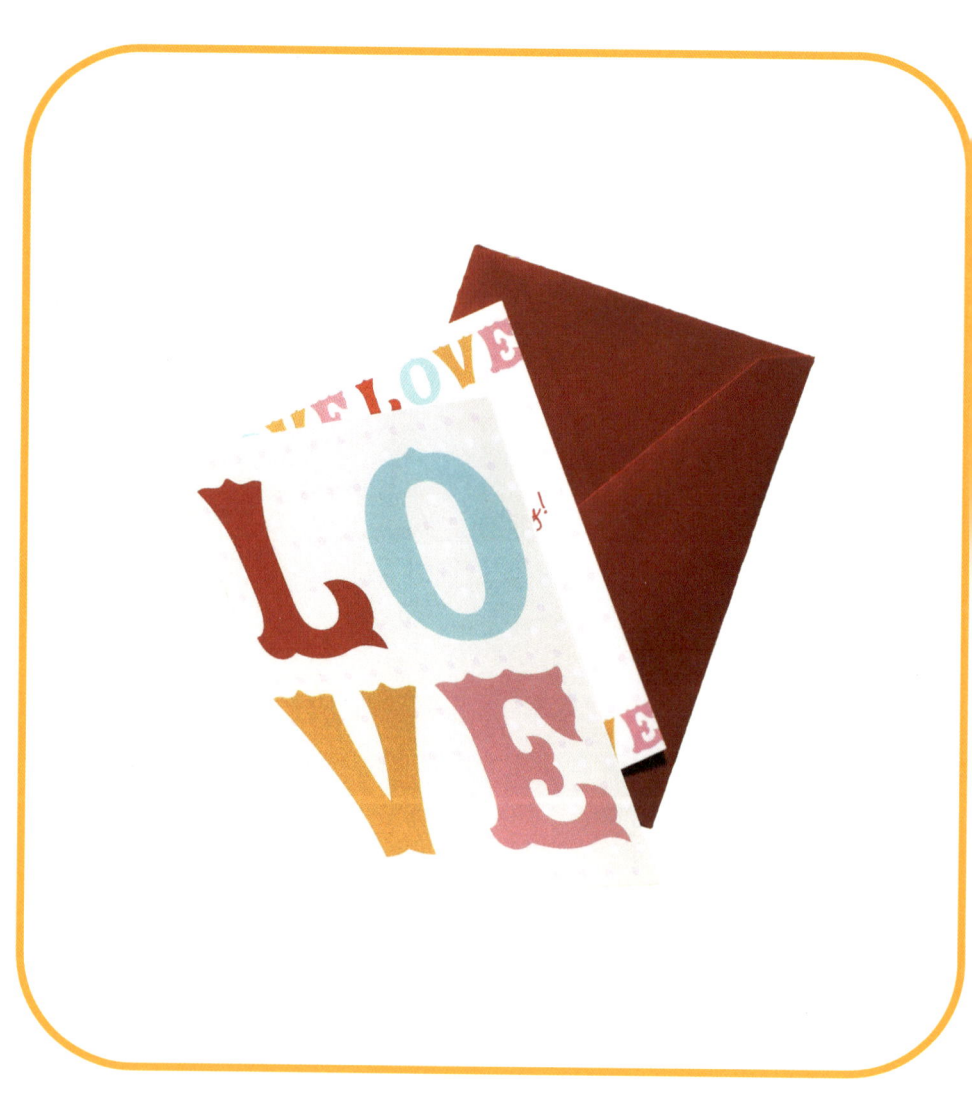

# card

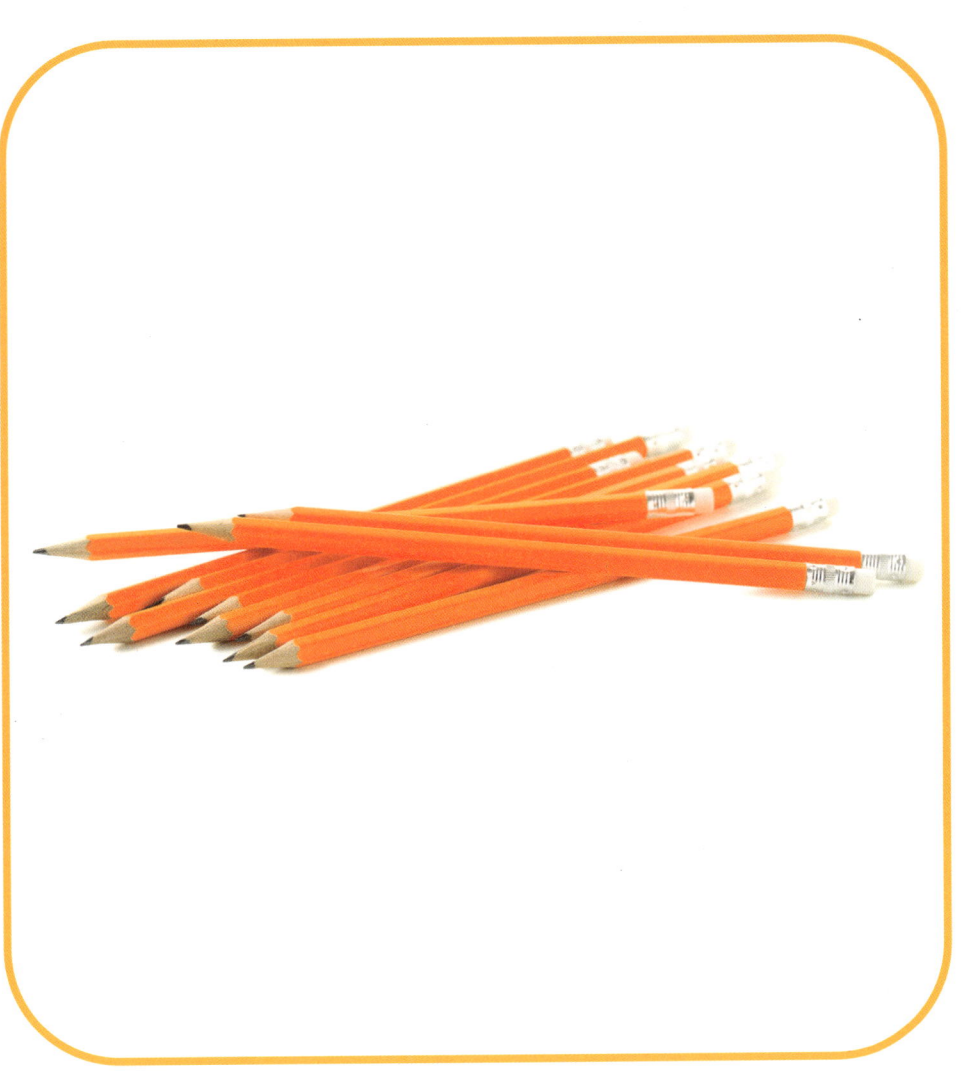

pencils

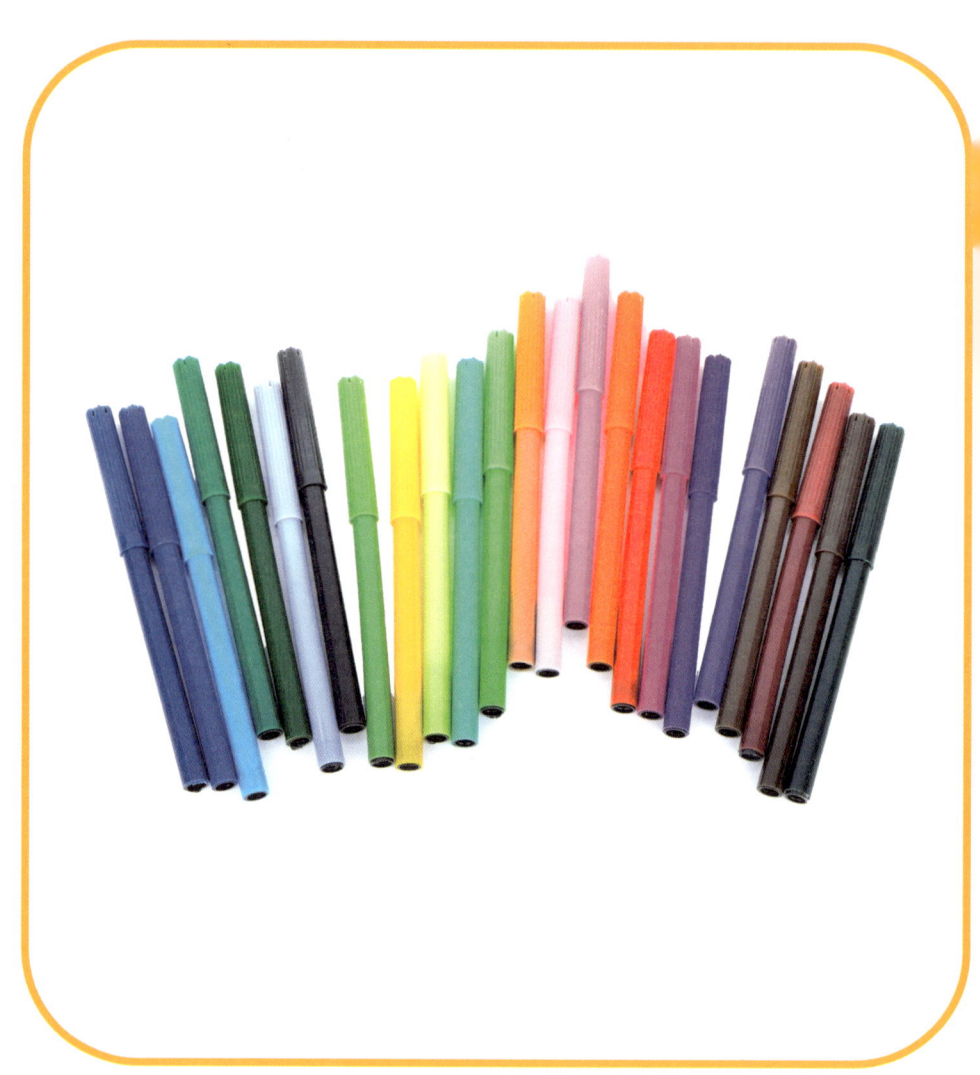

pens

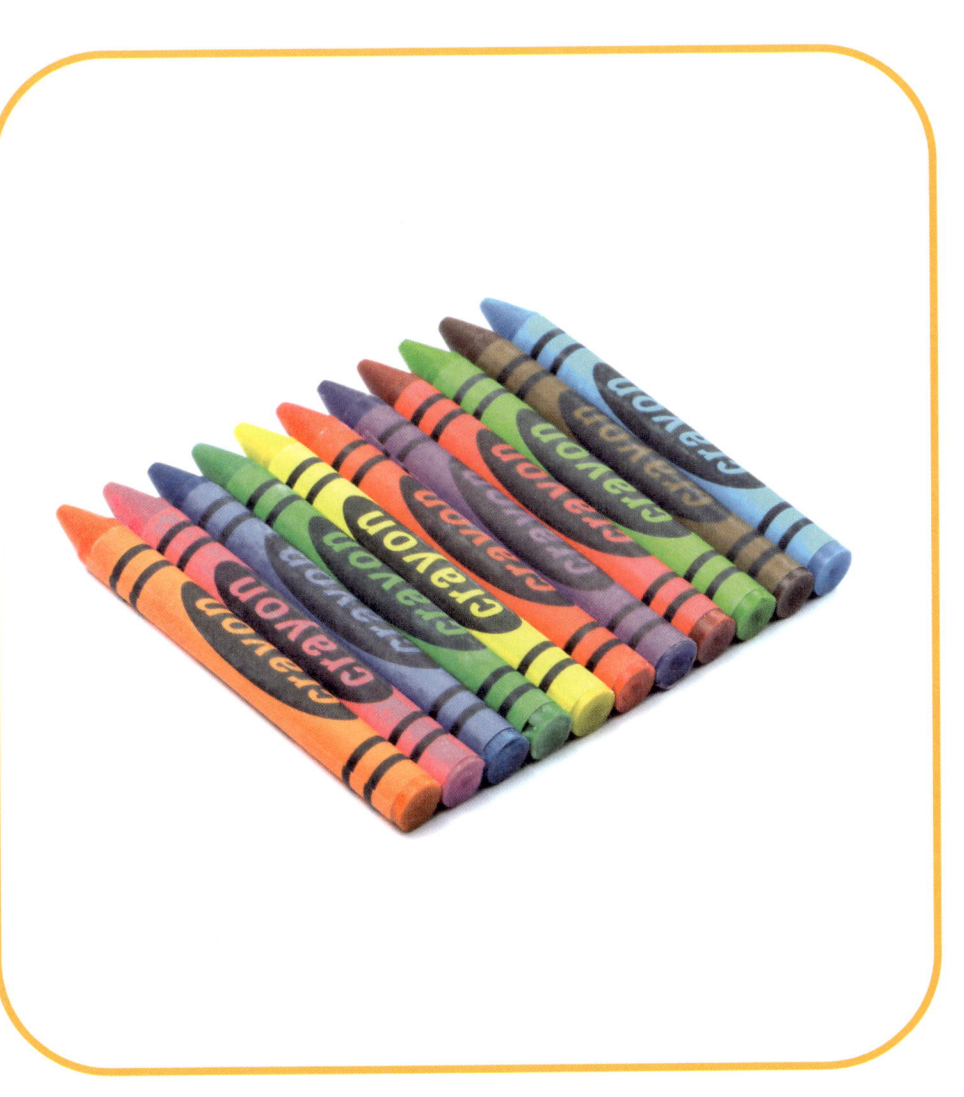

# crayons

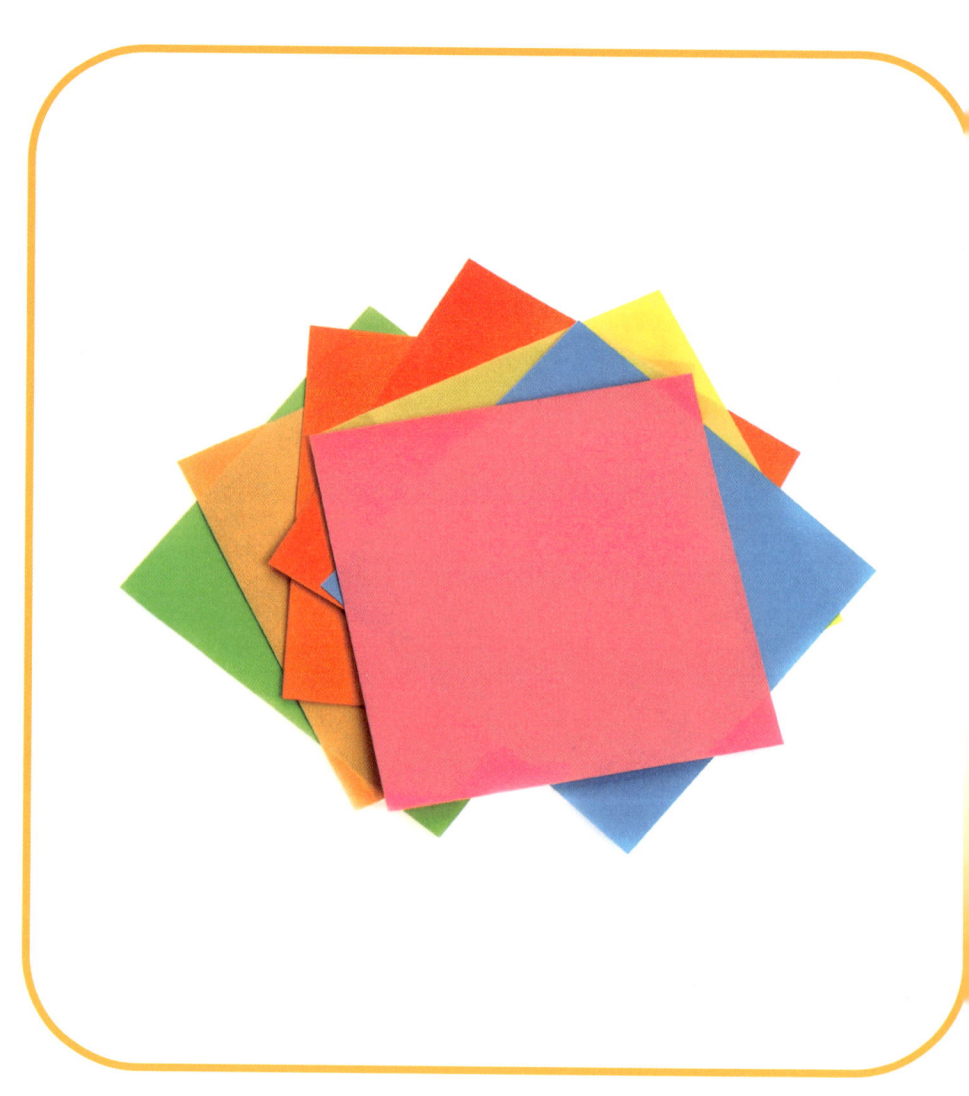

# Do you have paper?

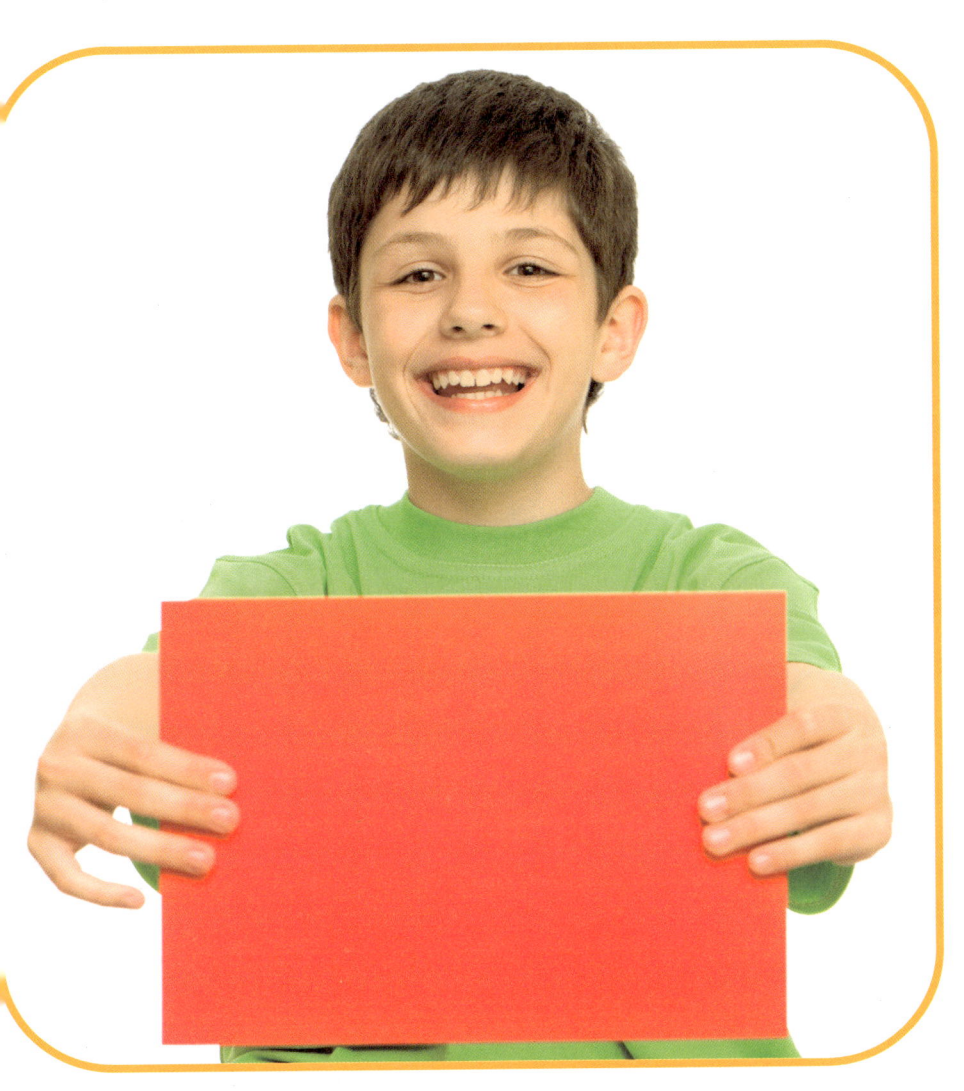

Yes, I do.

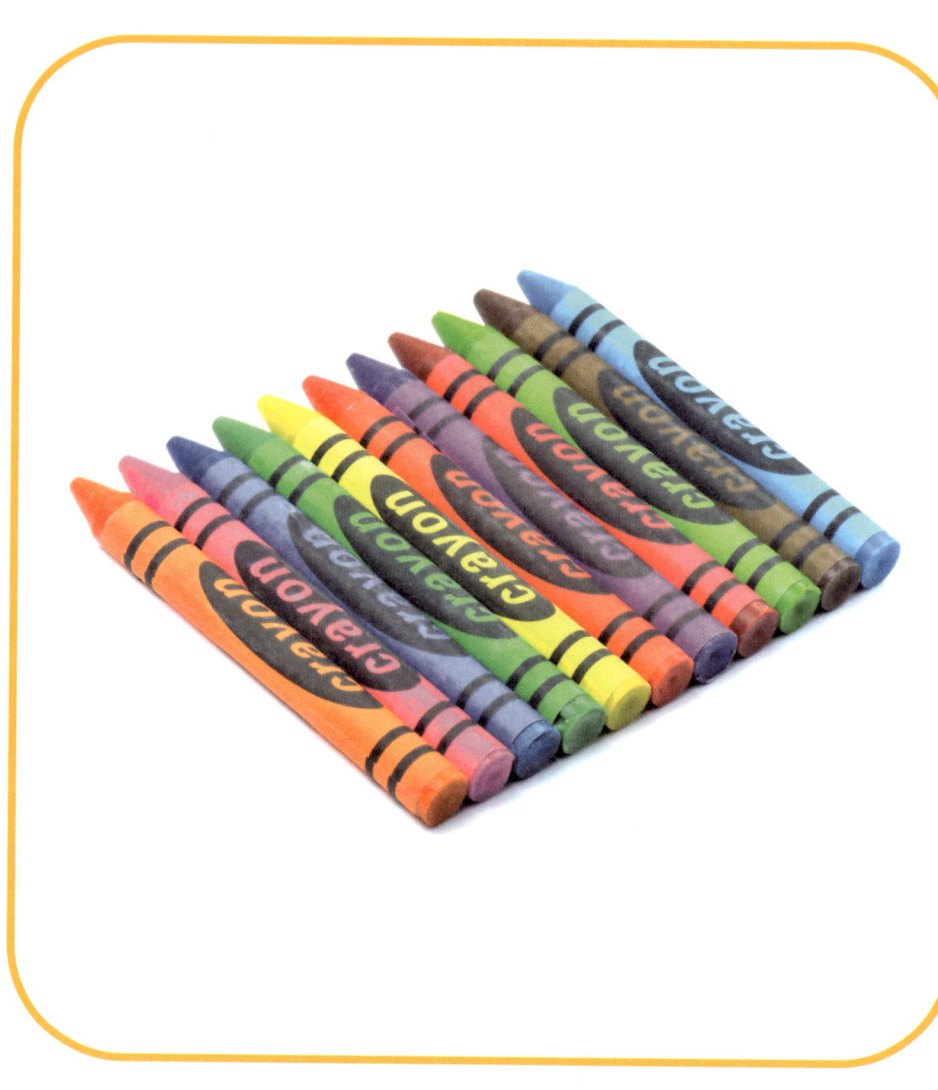

Do you have
crayons?

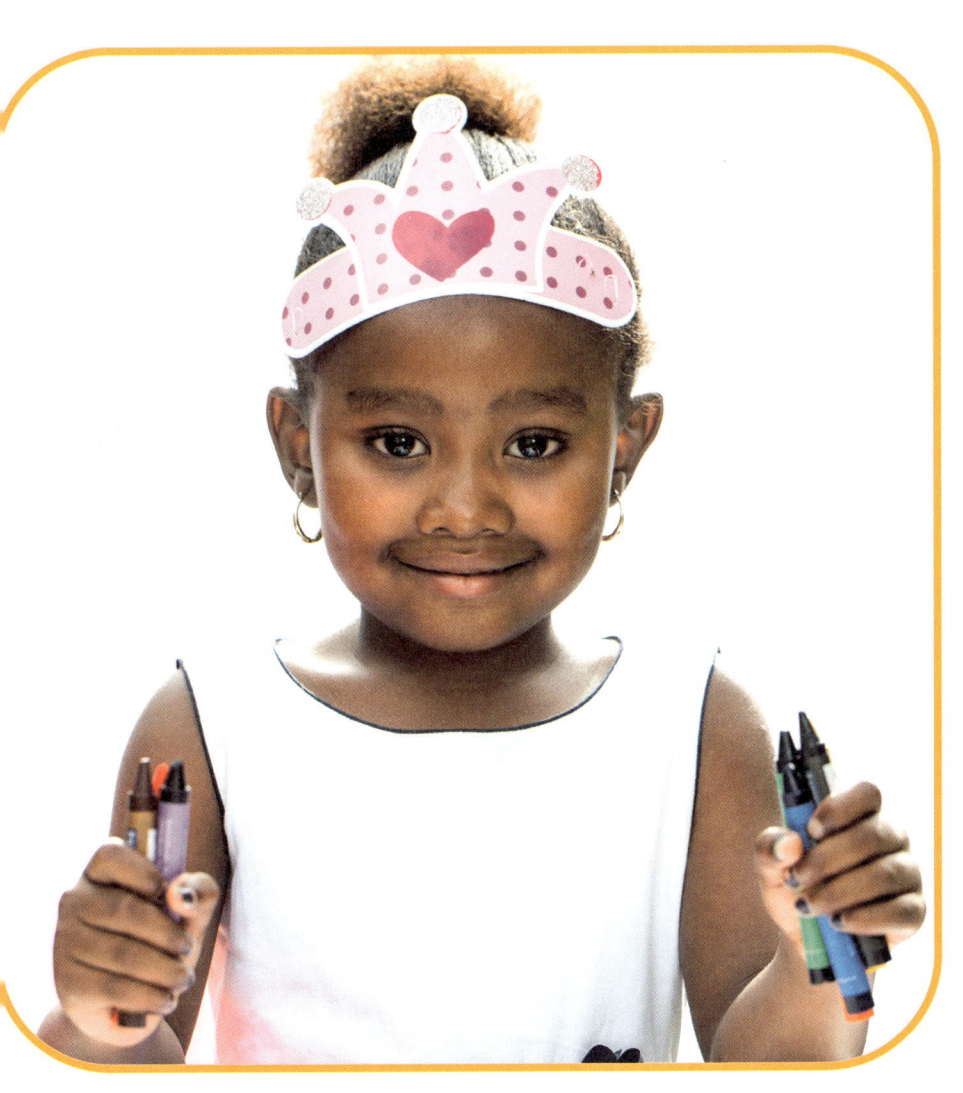

Yes, I do.

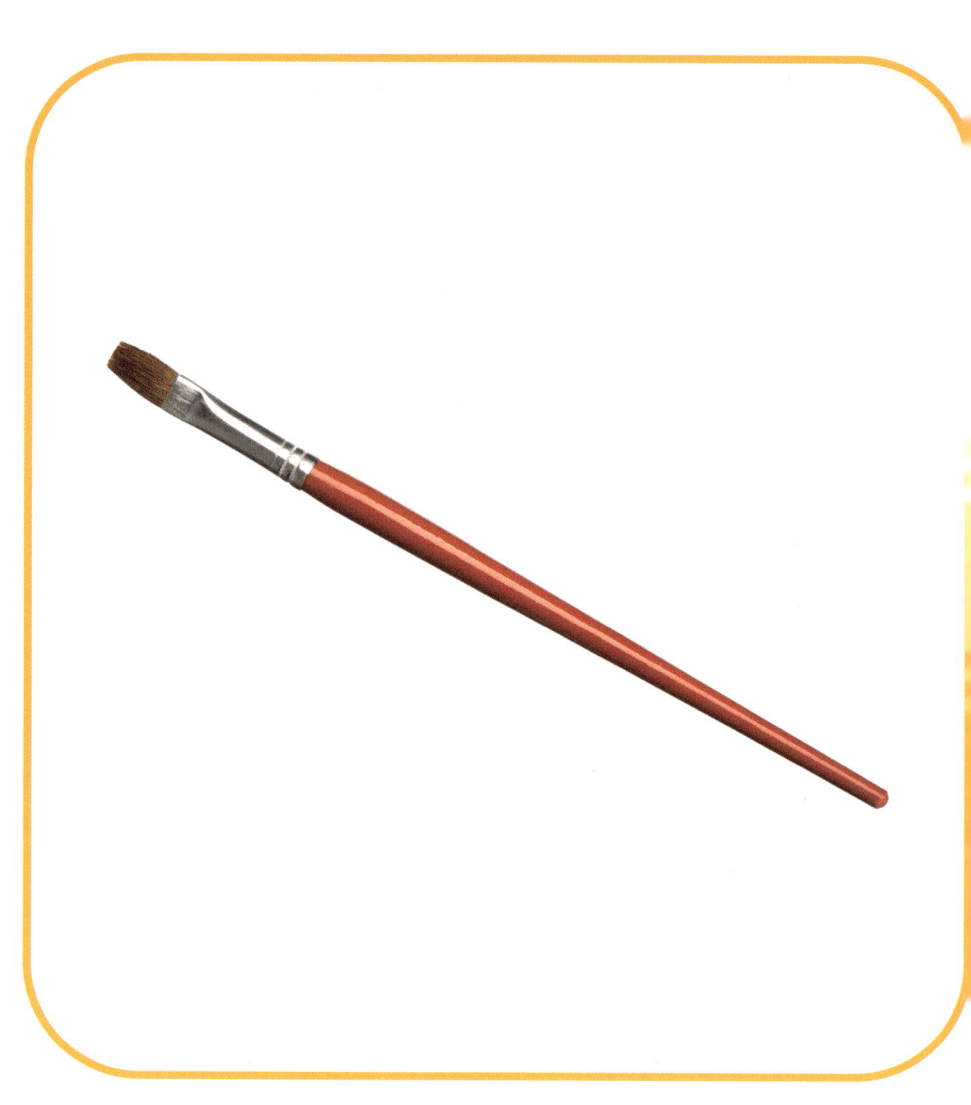

# Do you have a brush?

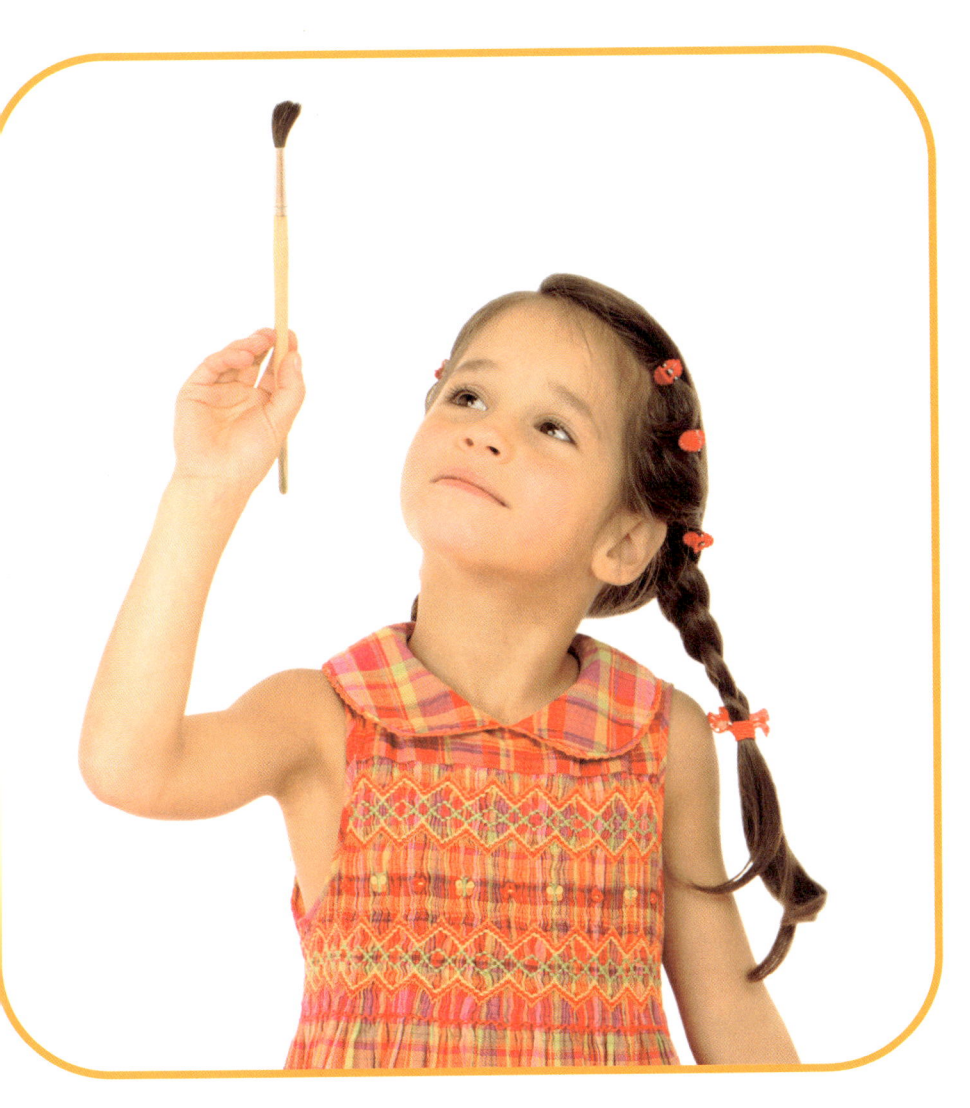

Yes, I do.

# Word List

paper

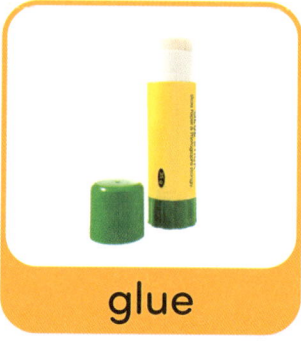
glue

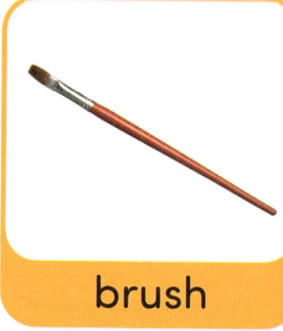
brush

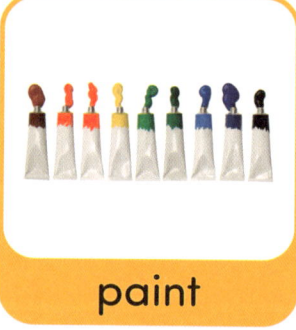
paint

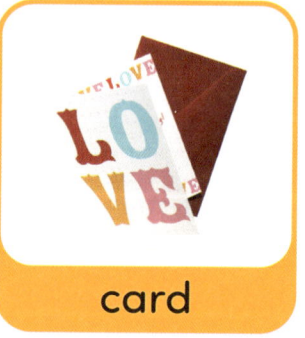
card

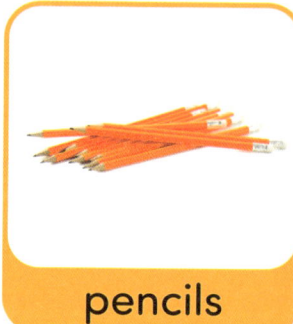
pencils

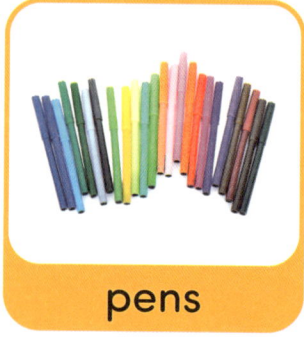
pens

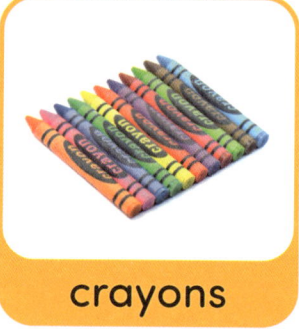
crayons